Let's Take a Trip

Yellowstone Park

by Frank Staub

photography by the author

Troll Associates

Library of Congress Cataloging-in-Publication Data

Staub, Frank J.
      Yellowstone Park / by Frank Staub; photography by the author.
           p.   cm.—(Let's take a trip)
      Summary: Describes the land, plants, and animals and their
interdependence at the world's oldest national park.
      ISBN 0-8167-1737-0 (lib. bdg.)   ISBN 0-8167-1738-9 (pbk.)
      1. Yellowstone National Park—Juvenile literature.   2. Natural
history—Yellowstone National Park—Juvenile literature.
[1. Yellowstone National Park.   2. Natural history—Yellowstone
National Park.   3. National parks and reserves.]   I. Title.
II. Series.
F722.S82   1990
917.87 '52—dc20   89-34371

The author and the publisher wish to thank the rangers at the Yellowstone National Park for their assistance and
cooperation, and to acknowledge Photo Researchers, Inc., The National Audubon Society, and the following for
their photographs: Harry Engels, p. 14; Tom Bledsoe, p. 15, St. Meyers/Okapia, p. 22; Francoise Gohier, p. 25;
Osames Summerhays/Science Source, p. 26 (top inset); and Vulcain/Science Source, p. 26 (bottom inset).

In Yellowstone National Park in Wyoming and parts of Montana and Idaho, the landscape is much the same as it has been for thousands of years. Broad valleys stretch out between wind-blown mountains, waterfalls thunder in the distance, and powerful rivers cut into the earth. Let's take a trip to Yellowstone and discover some of the secrets this natural wonderland holds.

Yellowstone is not only the world's oldest national park but also the largest national park outside Alaska. It is also an excellent place to see nature at work. Let's find out how the land, the animals, and the plants relate to each other and how, sometimes, the delicate balance of nature can be upset.

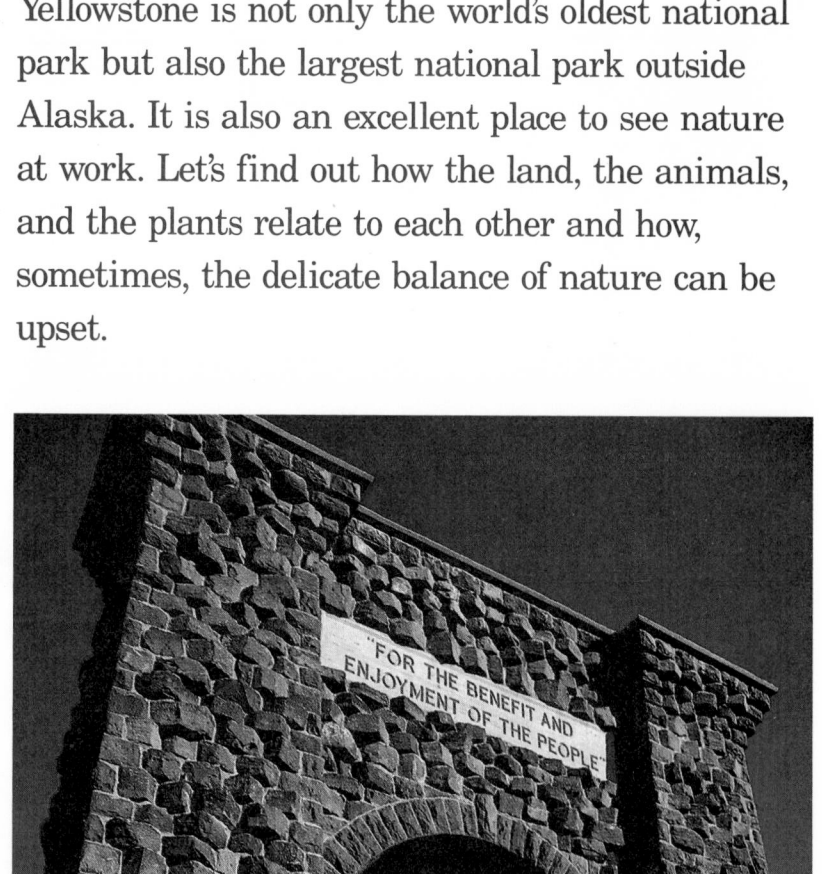

"FOR THE BENEFIT AND ENJOYMENT OF THE PEOPLE"

YELLOWSTONE NATIONAL PARK

CREATED BY ACT OF CONGRESS MARCH 1,1872

Many national parks have buildings, campgrounds, and paved roads that help visitors reach various parts of the park. But in Yellowstone, you can even take a ride on a stagecoach to visit sections of the park that may not be easily reached by car.

Two and a half million people visit Yellowstone each year. Park rangers remind them that they should not pick the flowers, collect the rocks, feed or hunt the animals, or litter the countryside. Helping to preserve the park is an important part of each ranger's job. The rangers also provide information about Yellowstone's many natural attractions, especially the animals.

Because Yellowstone's animals are protected from hunters, they have lost some of their fear of people. But they are still wild and should be watched only from a distance. Otherwise, they may become frightened and accidentally hurt someone.

One of Yellowstone's most common animals is the
American buffalo, or bison. Some forty million
bison once roamed North America. By 1889
reckless hunting had reduced the number of bison
to only 542. But thanks to places like Yellowstone,
where the animals are protected, the U.S. bison
population has now risen to over one hundred
thousand.

Bighorn sheep are not seen as often as bison because they prefer the high country, away from the roads. During the breeding season, male bighorn sheep, or rams, charge each other. The sound of their heads crashing together can be heard from far away.

Three kinds of deer live in Yellowstone. One species is called mule deer because they have large, mule-like ears—even when they are young. Mule deer have antlers that are shed each winter and grow back during the summer.

The other two kinds of deer found in Yellowstone are moose and wapiti, or American elk. American elk are larger than mule deer and have dark hair on their necks. Moose are the largest members of the deer family. Their long legs help them to walk through deep snow or wade through streams.

Pronghorn antelope are also found in Yellowstone. They are well-suited to flat areas where there are few trees. Pronghorn have large eyes to see long distances and strong legs to run away from danger.

One animal that lives in Yellowstone is rarely seen by visitors. White pelicans live and breed in a section of Yellowstone Lake that has been declared off limits to visitors. This was done so the birds wouldn't be disturbed.

Plants and animals interact in a delicate balance of nature in Yellowstone National Park. Plants use the energy in sunlight to grow. Animals eat the plants, and in turn, these animals are eaten by other animals. When plants and animals die, the chemicals in their bodies go back into the soil to nourish new plants.

Animals that eat other animals are called predators. The animals they eat are called prey. The snowshoe hare is the prey of several different predators, including the mountain lion and the coyote. The hare's coloring helps it hide by blending into the snowy landscape.

Forest fires caused by lightning are also part of the balance of nature in the park. After the trees are burned, more sunlight can reach the forest floor, allowing new plants to grow. These plants become a source of food for the animals.

Fires caused by lightning are often allowed to burn until they go out by themselves, or until the rain puts them out. However, when a forest fire threatens buildings and human life, fire fighting crews are sent out to keep it from spreading.

Sometimes human interference can upset the balance of nature. This happened in Yellowstone many years ago when hunters were allowed to kill the wolves that preyed on Yellowstone's elk population. At that time it was thought that eliminating the wolf would be good for the elk.

But with no wolves to keep the elk population under control, there were more and more elk. Soon there were so many elk that it became more and more difficult for them to find food, especially during the winter. Only then did people realize that the hunters had upset the natural balance between the number of wolves and the number of elk.

Bears have been known to prey on elk, but they usually eat smaller animals and plants. There are two kinds of bears in Yellowstone: black bears and grizzly bears. Black bears are smaller than grizzlies. In spite of their name, they are not always black.

Grizzly bears are big and powerful. They may be 7 feet long and weigh up to 850 pounds. One way to tell a grizzly from a black bear is by the hump on the grizzly's back. Scientists sometimes put radio collars on some of Yellowstone's grizzlies to track their movements. The collar transmits a signal that can be picked up several miles away and followed by a person with a tracking radio.

In the past, Yellowstone's bears waited for park visitors to give them food, rather than hunting for prey or finding berries in the wild. Garbage was put out to attract the bears, and visitors often fed them from parked cars. But although they appeared tame, the bears were still dangerous. Today the garbage dumps have been eliminated, and the bears no longer depend on park visitors for food.

Hikers in Yellowstone know that a surprised bear can be a dangerous bear. So they often have bells on their walking sticks to warn the bears that they are coming. Backpackers do everything they can to "bear-proof" their food. The best way is to hang it high in a tree for the night.

Firearms are not permitted in Yellowstone National Park. But sometimes grizzlies wander beyond the park's boundaries, where they are not as safe. Often, the grizzlies prey on cattle on the nearby ranches. To help protect their cattle, ranchers have fences on their land, and they keep a close watch on the herds.

During the winter, when food is scarce, bears go into a deep sleep that lasts for weeks at a time. Other animals, however, need to find food every day. Deer nibble on branches, and bison use their big heads to push snow away from the grass. Some of the park's animals move closer to Yellowstone's hot springs, where food is more readily available.

There are hot springs at Yellowstone because of magma. Magma is underground rock that has melted because it's so hot. When magma comes to the surface it is called lava. Thousands of years ago, volcanoes spewed lava onto the land. After the lava cooled and turned back into solid rock, some of it became yellow. That's how Yellowstone got its name.

Today, Yellowstone has plenty of hot, liquid rock several thousand feet beneath the surface. Water sinking into the earth from rain and melting snow is heated by the hot rock. Then it rises back to the surface, making Yellowstone a land of hot springs and steam.

The water temperature can be over 150 degrees Fahrenheit, so the park has provided boardwalks that let visitors get close to the springs without getting burned. The temperature in one of the springs at Yellowstone is cooler, because hot water mixes with cold river water. Swimming is permitted in this hot spring.

When the hot water is underground, minerals dissolve in it, just as sugar dissolves in hot tea. When the water comes to the surface it cools, and the dissolved minerals are deposited on the surface as a substance called *travertine*. Tons of travertine are deposited each day on the hot spring terraces and on Terrace Mountain.

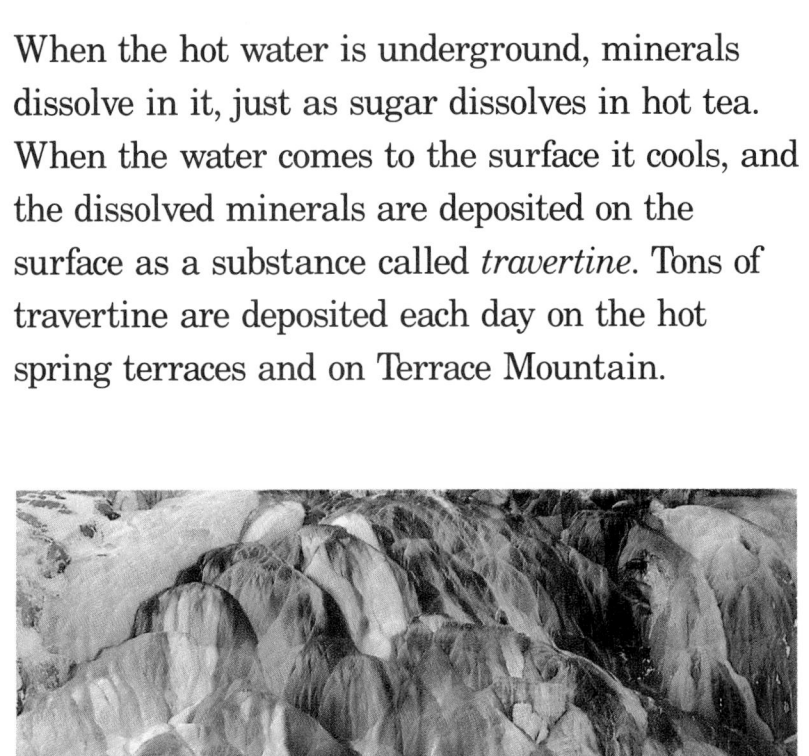

When the hot water and steam shoot out of the ground violently, *geysers* are formed. Some geyser eruptions last only a few minutes, while others last for hours. Some geysers erupt quite often. Old Faithful, Yellowstone's most famous geyser, is so named because it erupts regularly—approximately once every hour.

ERUPTION OF OLD FAITHFUL IS EXPECTED WITHIN FIVE MINUTES OF

Not all of Yellowstone's animals gather at the hot springs during the winter. Some migrate outside the park looking for food. But many nearby wintering grounds are now being logged, mined, or turned into housing developments. So it is becoming harder for some animals to find food.

Scientists now realize that to protect Yellowstone—its animals, its plants, and its land—the environment in and near the park must remain as natural as possible. This will take the cooperation of the people who run the park, those who visit it, and those who live and work nearby. After all, Yellowstone belongs to everyone, and everyone must help to preserve it.